TV **COOKS**

Nick Nairn

COOKS

Puddings

Published by BBC Worldwide Limited,
Woodlands, 80 Wood Lane,
London W12 0TT

The recipes in this book first appeared in the following:
Wild Harvest 2
© Nick Nairn 1997
Island Harvest
© Nick Nairn 1998

This edition first published 1999
© Nick Nairn 1999
The moral right of the author has been asserted

ISBN 0 563 38464 6

Photographs: Juliet Piddington
© BBC Worldwide Limited 1999

Commissioning Editor: Nicola Copeland
Project Editor: Charlotte Lochhead
Editor: Pam Mallender
Design: Town Group Creative
Stylist and Home Economist:
Sarah Ramsbottom
Author photograph: Graham Lees

Set in New Caledonia and Helvetica
Printed and bound in France by
Imprimerie Pollina S.A., Luçon, France
Colour separations by
Imprimerie Pollina S.A.
Cover printed by Imprimerie Pollina S.A.

Cover and frontispiece:
Cherry and Almond Tart

CONTENTS

RECIPE NOTES

Wash all fresh produce before preparation and prepare as necesssary.
Spoon measurements are level. Always use proper measuring spoons:
1 teaspoon = 5ml and 1 tablespoon = 15ml.
Never mix metric and imperial measures in one recipe. Stick to one or the other.
Nutritional notes are for a single serving when the dish is made for the number of servings stated in the recipe (unless indicated otherwise).
Eggs are large. If your kitchen is warm, keep the eggs in the fridge, but allow them to come to room temperature before using. While the proven risks of healthy people becoming ill from eating fresh raw eggs is minimal, pregnant women, the sick, the elderly and the very young should avoid eating raw or partially cooked eggs.

HANDY CONVERSION TABLES

Weight		Volume		Linear	
15g	½oz	30ml	1fl oz	5mm	¼in
20g	¾oz	50ml	2fl oz	10mm/1cm	½in
25g	1oz	100ml	3½fl oz	2cm	¾in
40g	1½oz	125ml	4fl oz	2.5cm	1in
55g	2oz	150ml	5fl oz (¼ pint)	5cm	2in
70g	2½oz	175ml	6fl oz	7.5cm	3in
85g	3oz	200ml	7fl oz (⅓ pint)	10cm	4in
100g	3½oz	225ml	8fl oz	13cm	5in
115g	4oz	250ml	9fl oz	15cm	6in
140g	5oz	300ml	10fl oz (½ pint)	18cm	7in
175g	6oz	350ml	12fl oz	20cm	8in
200g	7oz	400ml	14fl oz	23cm	9in
225g	8oz	425ml	15fl oz (¾ pint)	25cm	10in
250g	9oz	450ml	16fl oz	28cm	11in
280g	10oz	500ml	18fl oz	30cm	12in
350g	12oz	600ml	20fl oz (1 pint)		
375g	13oz	700ml	1¼ pints	**Oven Temperatures**	
400g	14oz	850ml	1½ pints	110C 225F GAS ¼	
425g	15oz	1 litre	1¾ pints	120C 250F GAS ½	
450g	1lb	1.2 litres	2 pints	140C 275F GAS 1	
550g	1¼lb	1.3 litres	2¼ pints	150C 300F GAS 2	
750g	1lb 10oz	1.4 litres	2½ pints	160C 325F GAS 3	
900g	2lb	1.7 litres	3 pints	180C 350F GAS 4	
1kg	2¼lb	2 litres	3½ pints	190C 375F GAS 5	
1.3kg	3lb	2.5 litres	4½ pints	200C 400F GAS 6	
1.8kg	4lb			220C 425F GAS 7	
2.25kg	5lb			230C 450F GAS 8	
				240C 475F GAS 9	

✳ **Suitable for freezing**

4

Somebody once said that every meal is a piece of theatre. You have the actors (the ingredients), the plot (the structure of your menu), and your willing audience (your guests), desperate to consume what you (the director) have choreographed for them. With this in mind, what better way to end a meal than with a grand finale – the pudding? The end of your meal is your chance to direct the closing scene, present it and sit back and soak in the applause. Okay, maybe I'm stretching the analogy just a wee bit, but the basic idea of food as theatre still holds.

Like any piece of theatre, the success of your meal lies in the direction and planning of the show. Not just planning what you're going to serve – how everything fits together, balancing tastes, colours and texture – but also planning the time you're going to spend in preparation. The bigger the meal, the easier the dishes should be to assemble and serve at the last minute. If you're serving a complex main course, the last thing you want to do is jump up and start whipping up a soufflé. The real advantage of the pudding course is that, if you want to plan your meal that way, you can do all the hard work in advance. All you then have to do is present your pudding to your delighted friends or family … and sit down, relax and enjoy the food and company.

In general, pastry and desserts are a more exact science than the rough and tumble of main courses, which is why it's better to give yourself plenty of time to take the care and attention that's needed to prepare them. There are four golden rules to follow, which make creating a great pudding simpler and a whole lot more enjoyable:

1 Read the recipe over a couple of times before you start and have the process in your mind. That way you won't be letting milk boil over while your head's buried in a cookery book.

2 Set the oven to the right temperature (if you're using it).

3 Make sure all the equipment you need is ready to be used, i.e. cake tins lined or soufflé dishes buttered and put in the fridge.

4 Finally measure and weigh out all your ingredients so that everything is sitting in front of you. Chefs call this *mis en place* and it's a great habit to get into, whatever you're cooking.

One last word of advice. The quality of any dish can only be as good as the quality of its ingredients. If you're cooking with chocolate get the good stuff, it costs more but it's worth it. If you're using fruit, choose the best of what's in season, and local, if you can it'll make all the difference. Oh and, by the way, theatre rules dictate that the director doesn't have to do the dishes!

Nick N

INGREDIENTS

Butter
I use unsalted butter for many of my puddings, plus I always keep some in the freezer – it freezes well. Many butter producers have come up with a piece of inspired packaging – they've marked 25g/1oz notches on the wrapper so that you know how much to cut without worrying about scales ... a touch of genius. If frozen, place butter overnight in fridge to defrost and remove from the fridge about 30 minutes before using if you need your butter softened.

Drambuie
Drambuie is not only my favourite post-prandial tipple, but the liqueur that I use most often in my cooking. There's just something in that combination of honey, spices and whisky that brings out or accentuates other flavours. The whisky with the history and mystery! Mine's a large one, thank you.

Eggs
If you can get your hands on eggs straight from a farm where the chooks run round free, you are in luck. The difference in quality between these eggs and even supermarket free-range eggs is huge: the yolks are a fantastic orange colour, and the flavour is something else. Once you've tried them, you'll never look back, and they are worth making the extra effort to find.

Figs
Figs are native to the Middle East and the Mediterranean coast and can be green, white, purple or black. All have sweet, juicy flesh full of tiny edible seeds and most have thin skins which are also edible. Look for firm unblemished fruit which just yields when you hold it in your hand without pressing it.

Mango
This large stone fruit grows all over the tropical and sub-tropical regions of the world. Ripe mangoes are very juicy with a yellow or orange skin and 'give' if gently squeezed. Avoid soft or shrivelled fruit.

Sugar
Natural brown sugar, such as muscovado, has much more flavour than white. It is a raw cane sugar available in light and dark varieties which is very soft, sticky and finely grained. Also keep icing, granulated and caster sugar in your storecupboard.

Vanilla pods
Vanilla pods are the dried, cured seed cases of an orchid plant, and are usually sold whole. If being used as a flavouring in milk or cream, the pod can be removed after being scalded in the liquid, washed, then dried and used again. And if you are just scraping out and using the seeds, place the pod in a jar of caster sugar to give a distinct vanilla flavour.

EQUIPMENT

Blowtorch
This is the perfect tool for finishing off crème brûlées, but you can, of course, get by with a very hot preheated grill. If you do decide to use a blowtorch, keep it away from children and take care when using it. Do not leave it alight and walk off to answer the phone or doorbell.

Chopping boards

Ten years ago the environmental health people said that we should use plastic chopping boards rather than wooden ones. Plastic boards are terrible! They blunt your knives and they retain the smell of food, so they taint what you're preparing. Now the health police have relented, thank goodness, but here are a couple of hints regarding wooden boards: wipe them down but don't put them in a dishwasher as they warp. A wet tea towel under the board when you're using it keeps it firmly in place and nice and level.

Crockery

It's much easier to make food look attractive on big white plates or in white dishes. Don't spend a fortune on crockery and have the food looking cluttered because of the pattern. Let the food speak for itself. Ramekins, great for soufflés, mousses and brûlées, can be made from porcelain, earthenware or glass and are usually sold in matching sets of four or six.

Electric whisk

A hand-held whisk gives you more control than a mixer when you're making things such as meringue. It's also easier to clean than a mixer and it saves your bulging, aching biceps from all the hard work needed when using wire balloon whisks.

Frying pans

The best frying pans are black iron. They are all-metal so can go in the oven. After being seasoned they are superb for cooking with – and they last for ever. As well as these you can get really good-quality stainless steel non-stick pans. Never buy a cheap non-stick pan because the non-stick surface will come off in bits in an outrageously short time, so buy the best you can afford.

Measuring jugs/spoons/scales

Plastic or metal measuring spoons are invaluable for measuring level tablespoons and teaspoons for successful results. And make sure your measuring jug is not only heatproof but also shows both metric and imperial measurements. Electronic scales are essential for precision measuring. Commercial kitchens wrap them loosely in plastic wrap and use them as normal. This stops all the debris in the kitchen getting into the gubbins of the scales.

Rolling pin

I prefer the polythene ones because they don't stick so much and don't dent so easily.

Seasoned baking sheet

Like pots and pans you should consider this as an investment – the more you bake with it the more like an old friend it will become. Treat it well and it will last for ever (or nearly).

Non-stick baking mats

Silpats or lift-offs are flexible silicon mats that chefs use for such things as brandy snaps and biscuits. You can now get something similar from cookshops and some supermarkets. Nothing sticks to the mat, but it won't stop things burning if you're not looking out for them!

Stirring essentials

A plastic spatula is ideal for scraping every little bit from mixing bowls and will pay for itself in months. Wooden spoons are a great asset when pushing food through sieves or stirring hot liquids in non-stick pans. And a large metal spoon is useful for mixing whisked egg whites into a mixture – it has a flatter edge than a wooden spoon resulting in less air being knocked out.

1 Bramley apples
2 Mango
3 Panettone
4 Plain chocolate
5 Icing sugar
6 Granny Smith apples
7 Red-skinned plums
8 Figs
9 Passion fruit
10 Blackberries
11 Blueberries
12 Redcurrants
13 Caster sugar
14 Light muscovado sugar
15 Dark muscovado sugar
16 White chocolate
17 Rhubarb
18 Hazelnuts
19 Muscatel raisins
20 Raspberries
21 Strawberries
22 Vanilla pods
23 Leaf gelatine
24 Ground almonds
25 Ground cinnamon
26 Cinnamon sticks
27 Cinnamon bark
28 Powdered gelatine
29 Fresh ginger

1. Baking tray
2. Baking sheet
3. Non-stick baking mats
4. Loaf tin
5. Measuring jug
6. Pastry brush
7. Measuring spoons
8. Dariole moulds
9. Frying pans
10. Spatula
11. Baking beans
12. Ramekins
13. Tartlet tins
14. Springform cake tin
15. Loose-bottomed cake tin
16. Loose-bottomed flan tin
17. Blowtorch
18. Scone cutters

Tarts

CHERRY AND ALMOND TART ❄

This has been one of our most successful puddings at the restaurant. The tart should be eaten warm, when the pastry will still be crumbly and light. Serve with cold Crème anglaise, otherwise known as custard! (page 62), or Cinnamon ice cream (page 59) to evoke memories of childhood puddings.

Serves 8–10

1 quantity Sweet pastry (page 62)

250g/9oz unsalted butter, softened

250g/9oz caster sugar

25g/1oz plain flour

250g/9oz ground almonds

4 eggs

600g can pitted black cherries, drained

3 tbsp apricot jam, to glaze (optional)

1 Preheat the oven to 200C/400F/Gas 6. Roll out the pastry to a 28cm/11in circle and use to line a 25cm/10in loose-bottomed flan tin. Fold the excess pastry over the top of the tin. Line with greaseproof paper and fill with baking beans, dried peas or butterbeans. Place on a baking sheet and chill for 15 minutes. Bake for 11 minutes, remove the lining paper and beans and bake for 9 minutes more until the pastry is lightly browned. Carefully trim off the overhanging pastry using a sharp knife. Reduce the oven to 160C/325F/Gas 3.

2 Cream the butter and sugar together in a large bowl until very pale and thick. Beat in the flour, then a quarter of the ground almonds with an egg until smooth. Repeat until all the almonds and eggs are incorporated.

3 Spread the almond frangipane mixture in the flan case right up the edge and over the pastry, then dot the cherries, here and there, over the top. Bake for 1 hour or until risen and golden.

4 If glazing, place the apricot jam in a small pan and leave to melt over a low heat. Add a little water if it is very thick. Press it through a sieve to remove any lumps, then brush liberally over the top of the tart to glaze. Serve warm.

Nutrition notes per serving for 8: *929 Calories, Protein 14g, Carbohydrate 77g, Fat 65g, Saturated fat 30g, Fibre 4g, Added sugar 39g, Salt 0.25g.*

❄ *The frangipane mixture can be successfully frozen for up to 6 weeks at the end of step 2 of the recipe. Wrap in plastic wrap and simply defrost in the fridge overnight.*

TIP

Instead of the cherries you can use other drained canned fruit such as apricots, peaches or pears, brambles or soft fresh fruit if you prefer.

FREE-FORMED APPLE TARTS

Serves 6

900g/2lb firm eating apples, such as Cox's or Egremont Russets, quartered, cored, peeled and thickly sliced

55g/2oz light muscovado sugar

1 tsp ground cinnamon

¼ tsp each of freshly grated nutmeg and ground cloves

1 quantity Sweet pastry (page 62)

1 egg white

2 tbsp semolina

2 tbsp caster sugar

1 Preheat the oven to 200C/400F/Gas 6. Lightly butter a baking sheet. Place the apple slices in a bowl and mix in the muscovado sugar and spices. Divide the pastry into six pieces, then roll each piece out on a lightly floured surface to an 18cm/7in circle.

2 Brush each circle with a little of the unbeaten egg white, then sprinkle one teaspoon of semolina into the centre of each one, leaving a 5cm/2in border around the edge. Pile the apple mixture into the centre of each circle, then fold the edges of the pastry over the fruit, leaving some of the fruit showing in the middle and pleating the pastry as you go to keep it in place.

3 Place on the baking sheet and chill for 30 minutes. Brush the edges of the tarts with more unbeaten egg white, then sprinkle with caster sugar. Bake for 25–30 minutes until the pastry is golden and the apples are cooked.

Nutrition notes per serving: *542 Calories, Protein 6g, Carbohydrate 76g, Fat 26g, Saturated fat 16g, Fibre 4g, Added sugar 23g, Salt 0.22g.*

MINCEMEAT TART

Serves 8

225g/8oz luxury mixed dried fruit, such as figs, prunes, dates, apricots and raisins, cut into raisin-sized pieces

400g jar mincemeat

juice and finely grated zest of 1 orange

1 Granny Smith apple, peeled, cored and grated

25g/1oz sugar

50ml/2fl oz dark rum

2 quantities Sweet pastry (page 62)

caster sugar, for dusting

1 Stir the dried fruit into the mincemeat with the orange juice and zest, apple, sugar and rum. If possible, cover and leave for 2–3 days to allow the mixture to absorb the orange juice and rum.

2 Preheat the oven to 200C/400F/Gas 6. Roll out half the pastry on a lightly floured surface and use to line a 25cm/10in loose-bottomed flan tin. Spoon in the mincemeat mixture and lightly level the top. Roll out the remaining pastry to a 28cm/11in circle. Brush the edge of the pastry case with a little water, lay the remaining pastry on top and press the edges together well to seal. Trim away excess pastry.

3 Prick the top here and there with a fork, then bake for 30–35 minutes or until pale golden. Dust with caster sugar and cut into wedges before serving warm.

Nutrition notes per serving: *852 Calories, Protein 8g, Carbohydrate 118g, Fat 40g, Saturated fat 25g, Fibre 4g, Added sugar 24g, Salt 0.48g.*

TIP

You could use the pastry to line individual tartlet tins instead and bake them for 10–15 minutes. Do look for good quality ready-to-eat dried fruit, so you'll have a rich moist filling.

TARTE TATIN

The love affair between the flavour of bananas and rum has always been intense; they belong together, especially in a dish like this where the bananas are glossy with sticky-sweet caramelised juices and the rum is infused in cool, freshly whipped cream.

Serves 6

85g/3oz caster sugar

55g/2oz unsalted butter

4 large bananas, peeled and thickly sliced on the diagonal

350g/12oz puff pastry or 1 ready rolled sheet

flour, for dusting

FOR THE RUM CREAM

1 tbsp light muscovado sugar

2 tbsp dark rum, or to taste

300ml/½ pint double cream

pinch of ground cinnamon, to decorate

1   Preheat the oven to 190C/375F/Gas 5. Place the sugar and butter in a 25cm/10in non-stick ovenproof frying pan. Cook over a medium heat, stirring from time to time, until the mixture turns into a smooth caramel. It will look very grainy to start with and the butter will look as if it has split away from the sugar, but just keep stirring and it will gradually come together. Remove the pan from the heat and make sure the caramel covers the base in an even layer.

2   Arrange the banana slices randomly over the base of the pan, overlapping here and there, so that they cover the caramel in a thick layer. Cut or roll out the pastry into a 28cm/11in circle – don't worry about it being too neat. Lay the pastry over the bananas and carefully tuck the edges down into the pan using a fork. Prick the top of the pastry, then bake for 30 minutes until the pastry is risen and golden. Leave to rest in the pan for 10 minutes.

3   Meanwhile, make the rum cream. Mix the sugar with the rum until the sugar has dissolved. Whip the cream until it begins to show signs of thickening, then whisk in the sweetened rum until it forms soft peaks. Cover and chill until ready to serve.

4   Run a sharp knife around the pastry to make sure that all the edges are free and place an inverted plate over the top of the pan. Turn the two together, give it a little shake and remove the pan. Cut the tart into six wedges and serve with the rum cream, sprinkled with cinnamon.

Nutrition notes per serving: *683 Calories, Protein 6g, Carbohydrate 65g, Fat 45g, Saturated fat 20g, Fibre 1g, Added sugar 18g, Salt 0.51g.*

VARIATIONS

For Mango Tarte Tatin: make the tart in the same way, using 1 very large or 2 smaller ripe, firm mangoes. Peel the mangoes, then slice the fruit away from either side of the the the thin flat stone in 2 whole pieces. Place the slices of fruit, cut-side down, on a board and slice into long 1cm (½in) thick slices. Cut away any bits of fruit left on the stone and use to fill any gaps in the pan. Serve with crème fraîche.

For Fresh Fig Tarte Tatin: make the tart in the same way, using 8 fresh ripe figs, halved. Serve with fromage blanc or fromage frais.

BUTTERSCOTCH TART

1 quantity Sweet pastry (page 62)

55g/2oz butter, softened

85g/3oz light muscovado sugar

55g/2oz granulated sugar

140g/5oz golden syrup

300ml/½ pint double cream, plus extra for serving (optional)

1 tsp vanilla extract

4 eggs

1   Use the pastry to line a 25cm/10in flan tin, and cook as in Step 1 above. Reduce the oven to 150C/300F/Gas 2.

2   Make the filling: place the butter, both sugars and the golden syrup in a pan. Stir over a low heat until the sugars have dissolved, then cook gently for 5 minutes until smooth and thick. Remove from the heat and stir in the cream and vanilla extract. Leave to cool for 10 minutes, then beat in the eggs.

3   Strain the mixture into the pastry case and bake for 35–40 minutes until just set. Leave to cool for 30 minutes. Cut into wedges and serve with lightly whipped double cream if liked.

Nutrition notes per serving: *676 Calories, Protein 7g, Carbohydrate 65g, Fat 45g, Saturated fat 27g, Fibre 1g, Added sugar 39g, Salt 0.51g.*

WALNUT AND WHISKY TARTS

Serves 6

1 quantity Sweet pastry (page 62)

70g/2½oz butter, softened

85g/3oz light muscovado sugar

2 eggs

175ml/6fl oz golden syrup

1½ tbsp whisky

pinch of salt

115g/4oz walnut pieces

1½ tbsp plain flour

115g/4oz walnut halves, to decorate

Athol brose cream, to serve (See Tip)

1   Preheat the oven to 200C/400F/Gas 6. Use the pastry to line six 10cm/4in tartlet tins. Fold the excess pastry over the top of the tins. Line with foil or greaseproof paper and fill with baking beans. Place on a baking sheet and chill for 15 minutes. Bake for 11 minutes, remove the lining paper and beans and bake for 9 minutes until the pastry is lightly browned. Carefully trim off the overhanging pastry using a sharp knife. Reduce the oven to 180C/350F/Gas 4.

2   Beat the butter and sugar together until pale and fluffy. Beat in the eggs, one at a time, then slowly mix in the syrup, whisky and salt. Mix the walnut pieces with the flour, then fold into the egg mixture. Pour into the pastry cases and bake for 10 minutes until the filling is lightly set and a thin crust has formed over the surface. Lower the oven to 160C/325F/Gas 3.

3   Arrange a ring of walnut halves around the outside edge of each tart, return to the oven and bake for 10 minutes until completely set. Serve warm with the athol brose cream.

Nutrition notes per serving: *937 Calories, Protein 13g, Carbohydrate 84g, Fat 62g, Saturated fat 24g, Fibre 3g, Added sugar 47g, Salt 0.82g.*

TIP

For the Athol brose cream: whisk 150ml /¼ pint double cream until it begins to thicken. Slowly whisk in 1½ tablespoons clear honey, preferably heather, then 50ml/2fl oz whisky until the mixture forms soft peaks.

Meringues

MUSCOVADO SUGAR MERINGUES WITH
LIME CREAM AND MANGOES

When I was wee, meringues were a huge treat and I still insist on serving these up in the restaurant in big paper cases. It reminds me of a time when the thought of a meringue after tea would occupy my thoughts all day.

Serves 6

3 egg whites

175g/6oz light muscovado sugar, sieved, plus a little extra for sprinkling (See Tip)

3 small ripe but firm mangoes

6 fresh mint sprigs, to decorate

FOR THE LIME CREAM

300ml/½ pint double cream

finely grated zest of 2 limes

3 tbsp fresh lime juice (about 1½ limes)

1 tbsp caster sugar

1 Preheat the oven to 110C/225F/Gas¼. Line a large baking sheet with non-stick baking paper or use a non-stick mat (page 7). Whisk the egg whites in a large, very clean bowl until they form stiff peaks. Very gradually whisk in the sugar, a spoonful at a time, making sure that you whisk the mixture well between each addition to ensure that the sugar has dissolved and combined with the egg whites. This is important to prevent the meringues from losing all their volume as muscovado sugar is quite moist and heavy.

2 Spoon the mixture into 6 meringue shapes on the baking sheet, then sprinkle the tops with a little more sugar. Bake for a minimum of 4 hours until very dry and hard. Cool and set aside.

3 Peel the mangoes, then slice the flesh away from either side of the thin flat stone in the centre. Cut each piece lengthways into long thin strips. Make the lime cream: whip the cream with the lime zest, lime juice and sugar until it forms stiff peaks. Spoon a little of the cream into the centres of six plates, arrange mango slices on top like the points of a star, then spoon on the remaining cream. Place a meringue in the centre of each star and decorate with the mint.

Nutrition notes per serving: *413 Calories, Protein 3g, Carbohydrate 49g, Fat 24g, Saturated fat 15g, Fibre 3g, Added sugar 33g, Salt 0.13g.*

TIP

It's important to use good-quality muscovado sugar here, and not that stuff which is just refined white sugar with a coating of molasses. I like Billington's sugars the best. Whatever you use, make sure you sieve it so that there are no lumps before you add it to the egg whites.

HAZELNUT PAVLOVA CAKE WITH RASPBERRY CREAM

A nutty Pavlova layered up with raspberries and whipped cream and dusted with icing sugar certainly looks the part. It does need the fruit syrup to provide extra juice and zing, though.

Serves 12

225g/8oz shelled hazelnuts (See Tip)

300g/10½oz egg whites (8–10 eggs)

450g/1lb caster sugar

2 tbsp balsamic vinegar

2 heaped tsp cornflour

450ml/16fl oz double cream

3 tbsp eau de framboises, eau de vie or Kirsch (See Tip, page 40)

3 tbsp icing sugar, plus extra for dusting

350g/12oz fresh raspberries

FOR THE RED FRUIT SYRUP

125ml/4fl oz Stock syrup (page 62)

225g/8oz prepared mixed summer fruits such as strawberries, raspberries, blackberries, redcurrants and blackcurrants

1   Preheat the oven to 180C/350F/Gas 4. Grease and base-line two 30cm/12in springform cake tins with baking paper. Spread the hazelnuts on a baking sheet and roast for 10 minutes or until richly golden. Cool, then tip into a clean tea towel and rub off the skins. Transfer to a food processor and give them a quick blitz for a few seconds until finely ground. Reduce the oven to 160C/325F/Gas 3.

2   Whisk the egg whites in a bowl until they form soft peaks. Continue whisking, adding the sugar a spoonful at a time. Make sure you mix the sugar thoroughly into the egg whites before you add the next spoonful. When all the sugar has been added, mix the balsamic vinegar with the cornflour and whisk into the whites for 6–8 minutes until the meringue is very thick and shiny.

3   Fold the ground hazelnuts into the meringue mixture, divide it evenly between the tins and level with the back of a spoon. The mixture should be no more than 2cm/¾in thick. Bake for 30 minutes until they have risen and are lightly browned on top. Leave to cool in the tins for 2 hours before removing.

4   Meanwhile, make the red fruit syrup. Bring the stock syrup up to a simmer in a small pan. Add the summer fruits and cook gently for 15–20 minutes. Transfer to a liquidiser or food processor and blend until smooth. Strain through a fine sieve into a bowl and leave to cool, then cover and chill in the fridge until needed.

5   To assemble the pavlova, whip the cream with the eau de framboises and icing sugar into soft peaks. Gently fold in the raspberries so that they break up very slightly and the cream thickens a little more. Sandwich the two meringues together with the cream, transfer to a plate and leave in the fridge for 4 hours to firm up. Serve cut into 12 wedges, dusted with icing sugar and with the red fruit syrup drizzled round the edges of the plate.

Nutrition notes per serving: *526 Calories, Protein 6g, Carbohydrate 59g, Fat 30g, Saturated fat 12g, Fibre 2g, Added sugar 53g, Salt 0.17g.*

TIP

Ground nuts give a firmer texture and good, nutty flavour when added to the mix of a basic pavlova. If you like, you could use pistachios instead of hazelnuts – these will give a lush green tinge to the finished meringue.

Soufflés

HOT PASSION FRUIT SOUFFLÉS

I like to make these little soufflés using 3–4 passion fruit for each one so that you get a really sherbety taste, but you could cut the number of fruit by half and make the 'jam' with just 25g/1oz caster sugar if you wish. These seem to rise higher than any other soufflé I know.

Serves 6

24 passion fruit, halved and pulp scooped out

190g/6½oz caster sugar, plus extra for dusting and to serve

butter, for greasing

350ml/12fl oz milk

3 egg yolks

15g/½oz cornflour

15g/½oz plain flour

6 egg whites

1   Place the passion fruit pulp in a pan, add 55g/2oz of the sugar and stir over a gentle heat until the sugar has dissolved. Bring to the boil, then boil rapidly for 10 minutes, stirring frequently, towards the end of cooking, until you are left with a thick 'jam'. Strain through a sieve to remove the seeds and set aside.

2   Preheat the oven to 200C/400F/Gas 6. Slide a baking sheet on to the middle shelf. Lightly butter six 7.5cm/3in ramekins and dust with a little caster sugar.

3   Pour all but one tablespoon of the milk into a pan and bring slowly to the boil. Meanwhile, beat the egg yolks, 40g/1½ oz of the sugar, all the cornflour, plain flour and reserved milk together in a bowl until smooth. Whisk in the hot milk, return the mixture to the pan and bring to the boil, stirring. Reduce the heat and simmer very gently for 10 minutes, beating it every now and then, until you have cooked out the taste of the flour.

4   Transfer to a bowl and beat in the passion fruit jam. Whisk the egg whites into soft peaks, then whisk in the remaining caster sugar. Lightly whisk a quarter of the whites into the custard to loosen it slightly, then carefully fold in the remainder. Spoon into the ramekins, level the tops, then run the tip of a knife around the inside edge of each dish to release the mixture.

5   Slide the ramekins on to the baking sheet and bake for 10–12 minutes until the soufflés are well risen, browned and doubled in height but still slightly wobbly. Quickly lift on to small dessert plates, sprinkle with caster or icing sugar and serve straight away before they have time to sink.

Nutrition notes per serving: *287 Calories, Protein 10g, Carbohydrate 44g, Fat 9g, Saturated fat 4g, Fibre 2g, Added sugar 33g, Salt 0.32g.*

TIP

As with all soufflés, butter the moulds well and don't overwhisk the egg whites. If you are tempted to open the oven door to see how they are doing, don't slam it shut.

APPLE SOUFFLÉS WITH APPLE SORBET ❋

There are two very different flavours at work here. The intense, cooked flavour of the soufflé and the light zing of the sorbet. The sorbet is one of the easiest puddings you'll ever make and probably one of the cleverest.

Serves 6

4 Cox's apples, peeled, cored and diced

125ml/4fl oz cider

2 tbsp Calvados (See Tip, page 28)

300ml/½ pint milk

3 egg yolks

70g/2½ oz caster sugar, plus extra for dusting

15g/½ oz cornflour

15g/½ oz plain flour

4 egg whites

FOR THE SORBET

4 Granny Smith apples, cored and diced

juice of 1 lemon

90ml/3fl oz Stock syrup (page 62)

1 Make the sorbet: toss the apple pieces in one tablespoon of the lemon juice, then spread over a baking sheet and freeze for 1–1½ hours, until hard. Remove from the freezer and leave to thaw slightly at room temperature for 10 minutes. Scrape into a food processor, add the remaining lemon juice and the Stock syrup and process until smooth. Transfer to a freezerproof box, cover and freeze for 3–4 hours until firm. Soften in the fridge for 10 minutes before eating.

2 Place the apples, cider and Calvados in a pan and cook for 30 minutes over a low heat, beating with a wooden spoon now and then if necessary, until most of the liquid has evaporated and you are left with a very thick purée. Set aside.

3 Preheat the oven to 220C/425F/Gas 7. Lightly butter six 7.5cm/3in ramekins, dust with a little caster sugar and chill in the fridge.

4 Bring the milk to the boil in a pan. Meanwhile, beat the egg yolks, 40g/1½oz of the caster sugar, all the cornflour and plain flour together in a bowl until smooth. Whisk in the hot milk, then return the mixture to the pan and bring back to the boil, stirring. Reduce the heat and simmer gently for 10 minutes. Pour into a large heatproof bowl and stir in the apple purée.

5 Whisk the egg whites to soft peaks, then very gradually whisk in the remaining caster sugar to make a soft meringue. Stir a quarter of the meringue into the apple custard to loosen it slightly, then very gently fold in the remainder. Spoon into the ramekins and bake for 12–13 minutes until brown but still slightly wobbly. The mixture won't double in height because of the extra weight of the apple. Serve immediately with a scoop of sorbet.

Nutrition notes per serving: *232 Calories, Protein 6g, Carbohydrate 43g, Fat 5g, Saturated fat 2g, Fibre 2g, Added sugar 24g, Salt 0.20g.*

❋ *The sorbet keeps well in the freezer for up to 2 weeks. Leave in the fridge for 10 minutes before eating.*

TIP

Leaving the bright, deep green skins on the Granny Smith apples will give the sorbet a lovely pastel colour, while their tart and only moderately sweet flesh provides a refreshing zing.

Hot Favourites

PANETTONE AND BUTTER PUDDING

Panettone, a rich Italian fruit bread often served as a Christmas treat, gives a classic pudding a new lease of life. Trawl your local delicatessen for a January bargain. It doesn't matter if it's a little stale as the bread will be softened by the cream. However, it shouldn't be in any way heavy or eggy.

Serves 8

225g/8oz butter, melted

1 vanilla pod, split and seeds removed

300ml/½ pint double cream

300ml/½ pint milk

6 egg yolks

55g/2oz caster sugar

450g/1lb panettone, cut into 1cm/½in slices

2 tbsp light muscovado sugar

Crème anglaise, to serve (page 62)

1 Preheat the oven to 150C/300F/Gas 2. Grease a 900g/2lb loaf tin with some of the melted butter.

2 Place the vanilla pod and seeds in a pan with the cream and milk. Bring slowly to the boil, then remove from the heat and leave to infuse for 20 minutes. Whisk the egg yolks and caster sugar together in a bowl until pale and creamy. Reheat the cream and milk mixture, then lift the vanilla pod out of the pan, rinse and set aside to use again.

3 Whisk the hot cream and milk into the egg yolks. Return the mixture to the pan and cook over a gentle heat, stirring constantly, until it thickens enough to coat the back of a spoon.

4 Place a layer of panettone in the tin, trimming to fit, and pour over one-third of the melted butter. Leave for a few seconds to seep into the bread, then pour over one-third of the custard. Repeat twice more, then cover with the remaining panettone slices and sprinkle with the brown sugar. Leave to stand for 2 hours or until the panettone has absorbed all the custard. Place the loaf tin in a roasting tin and pour in enough boiling water to come halfway up the sides of the loaf tin. Bake for 45 minutes–1 hour until just set (test with a skewer). Lift the loaf tin out of the water and leave to cool slightly. Slice and serve on warm plates surrounded by the warm crème anglaise.

Nutrition notes per serving: *648 Calories, Protein 8g, Carbohydrate 42g, Fat 51g, Saturated fat 29g, Fibre 2g, Added sugar 11g, Salt 1.06g.*

TIP

Panettone has enough fruit for my taste, but you could add some raisins that have been soaked in rum or Calvados. Calvados is an apple brandy that takes its name from the centre of the Normandy apple orchards in France.

PLUM CLAFOUTIS

Serves 8

85g/3oz butter

10 ripe Victoria or red-skinned plums, halved and stoned

8 eggs

225g/8oz caster sugar, plus extra to serve

½ tsp salt

2 tbsp dark rum

400ml/14fl oz milk

225g/8oz plain flour

1 Preheat the oven to 200C/400F/Gas 6. Use 25g/1oz of the butter to grease a round, shallow 28cm/11in ovenproof baking dish. Place the plums in the dish cut-side down. Melt the remaining butter in a small pan.

2 Break the eggs into a large mixing bowl and add the sugar, salt, rum and milk. Whisk together, then gradually whisk in the flour and the melted butter. Pour the mixture through a sieve into the baking dish and bake for 40 minutes until well risen and golden brown. Dredge with caster sugar and serve immediately.

Nutrition notes per serving: *427 Calories, Protein 11g, Carbohydrate 60g, Fat 17g, Saturated fat 8g, Fibre 2g, Added sugar 30g, Salt 0.76g.*

TIP

Clafoutis is like a sweet toad-in-the-hole and is a traditional vehicle for cherries. It makes a nice late-summer pudding when the sweet Victoria plums are at their best. It keeps well and can be reheated in the microwave. Irresistible with a scoop of Cinnamon ice cream (page 59), you'll find it well worth a detour from any diet.

OATY RHUBARB CRUMBLES

Serves 6

900g/2lb rhubarb, trimmed and cut into 2.5cm/1in pieces

6 slices fresh root ginger

pared zest of 1 small orange

175g/6oz caster sugar

280g/10oz plain flour

140g/5oz butter, cubed

115g/4oz light muscovado sugar

85g/3oz rolled oats

Crème anglaise, to serve (page 62)

1 Preheat the oven to 200C/400F/Gas 6. Place the rhubarb, ginger, orange zest and sugar in a pan. Cover and cook over a gentle heat for a few minutes, stirring very gently every now and then, until the rhubarb is only just tender and still holding its shape. Tip the mixture into a sieve set over a small clean pan, discard the ginger and orange zest and leave the syrup to drain out of the rhubarb.

2 Meanwhile, sift the flour into a large bowl and rub in the butter until the mixture looks like fine breadcrumbs. Stir in two tablespoons of the brown sugar. Place six 10cm/4in lightly buttered metal pastry cutters or cooking rings on a baking sheet and spoon about two tablespoons of the flour and butter mixture into each one. Spread evenly, then press down very lightly with the back of the spoon. Stir the remaining brown sugar and rolled oats into the remaining crumble mixture.

3 Divide the rhubarb between each ring, level the tops, then cover with a layer of the crumble topping. Bake for 25–30 minutes until crisp and golden. Gently warm the rhubarb syrup. Slide a fish slice under each crumble and place on a warm serving plate. Carefully lift off the cutters or rings and pour round the syrup and warm crème anglaise.

Nutrition notes per serving: *603 Calories, Protein 8g, Carbohydrate 99g, Fat 22g, Saturated fat 13g, Fibre 5g, Added sugar 51g, Salt 0.51g.*

BANANA CRÊPES WITH RUM CREAM ❄

I don't need an excuse to make a feast of bananas and I defy you to eat many of these without needing a nap, or wheelchair to ferry you from the table. They're far from sensible, but that's what puddings are for. Try them with an Australian Liqueur Muscat to compound the effect.

Serves 8

55g/2oz butter

8 ripe bananas, cut into slices on the diagonal

4 tbsp dark muscovado sugar

1 tbsp fresh lemon juice

FOR THE CRÊPE BATTER

2 eggs

20g/¾oz caster sugar

250ml/9fl oz milk

100g/3½oz plain flour

20g/¾oz clarified butter (See Tip), melted, plus extra for cooking the crêpes

FOR THE RUM CREAM

2 tbsp dark muscovado sugar

50ml/2fl oz dark rum

1 ripe banana, chopped

300ml/½ pint double cream

1. Make the crêpe batter: break the eggs into a bowl and whisk in the sugar and half the milk. Whisk in the flour and melted butter until smooth, then gradually whisk in the remaining milk. Set aside, covered for 1 hour, to rest.

2. Heat a 15–18cm/6–7in heavy-based frying pan until hot. Brush with a little clarified butter, pour in some batter (about two tablespoons) and tilt the pan until the mixture covers the base in a thin, even layer – as soon as you've cooked a couple you will be able to judge how much you will need for the rest. Cook over a high heat for 1–2 minutes, until golden underneath, then lift up the edge with a palette knife, flip it over and cook for 30 seconds–1 minute until lightly browned. Tip out on to a plate and repeat, layering the crêpes up with squares of greaseproof paper, until you have made about 16.

3. Make the rum cream: place the sugar and rum in a small pan and bring to the boil, stirring. Add the chopped banana and simmer for 5 minutes, until the mixture has reduced and thickened. Stir in the cream and bring the mixture back to the boil. Blitz briefly with a hand-held blender until smooth, or strain through a fine sieve, then return to the pan and keep warm.

4. Preheat the oven to 180C/350F/Gas 4. Place the crêpes on a heatproof plate, cover with foil and heat through in the oven (or cover with plastic wrap and microwave) until hot. Melt the butter in a large frying pan or two smaller ones, add the banana slices in a single layer and fry over a high heat for 1–2 minutes on each side, until lightly browned. Sprinkle with the sugar and lemon juice and remove from the heat.

5. Spoon a few of the bananas on to a quarter of each crêpe. Fold the crêpe in half, then in half again to make a cone-shaped parcel. Repeat to make the other parcels. Place two crêpes in each serving bowl and spoon over the rum cream.

Nutrition notes per serving: *526 Calories, Protein 6g, Carbohydrate 59g, Fat 29g, Saturated fat 18g, Fibre 2g, Added sugar 14g, Salt 0.25g.*

❄ *The crêpes can be made in advance, layered with greaseproof paper and frozen, wrapped in foil. Defrost in the fridge as needed.*

TIP

To make clarified butter: melt 250g/9oz unsalted butter in a small pan over a low heat. Stand for a few minutes until all the oil rises to the top, then skim off the oil into a sealable plastic container. It will keep for 2 months.

CLOOTIE DUMPLING

A real Scottish dish and none the worse for that, traditionally made in an old pillowcase. Clotted cream is the perfect accompaniment.

Serves 8

225g/8oz plain flour, plus 25g/1oz for sprinkling

1 tsp bicarbonate of soda

1 tsp mixed spice

1 tsp ground cinnamon

1 tsp ground ginger

¼ tsp Maldon salt

175g/6oz caster sugar, plus 1 tbsp for sprinkling

115g/4oz shredded suet

115g/4oz sultanas

85g/3oz currants

85g/3oz stoned dates, chopped

55g/2oz muscatel raisins

1 apple or carrot, coarsely grated

1 tbsp black treacle

1 egg

150ml/¼ pint buttermilk

225g/8oz clotted cream, to serve

1 Sift the flour, bicarbonate of soda, spices and salt into a bowl and stir in the sugar, suet, dried fruits and the grated apple or carrot. Mix the treacle with the egg and add the buttermilk bit by bit, and mix into the dry ingredients to give a soft mixture with a cake-like dropping consistency.

2 Dip a large piece of muslin, an old pillowcase, a pudding cloth or a tea towel into boiling water, remove and squeeze out excess water. Lay it out on a surface and sprinkle a 30cm/12in circle in the centre with the 25g/1oz of flour and the tablespoon of caster sugar. Spoon the pudding mixture on top, then bring the opposite corners of the cloth together over the top and tie securely with string, leaving a little room for the pudding to expand.

3 Rest a large, heatproof plate in the base of a large pan on some sort of trivet or container so that it is not in direct contact with the heat and place the pudding on the plate, knotted side up. Pour in enough water to almost cover the pudding, cover with a tight-fitting lid and simmer gently for 3¾ – 4 hours. Take a peek every now and then to check the water level and top it up with boiling water if necessary.

4 Preheat the oven to 180C/350F/Gas 4. Lift the pudding out of the pan and dip it briefly in a bowl of cold water – this will ensure that the outside of the pudding does not stick to the cloth when you unwrap it. Undo the parcel, fold back the cloth and invert the pudding on to an ovenproof serving plate. Slide it into the oven and leave for 15 minutes or until the outside of the pudding has dried off. Serve in chunky wedges with the clotted cream and perhaps a small glass of whisky.

Nutrition notes per serving: *467 Calories, Protein 6g, Carbohydrate 85g, Fat 14g, Saturated fat 6g, Fibre 2g, Added sugar 27g, Salt 0.76g.*

TIP

I recently judged a clootie dumpling competition and I learned that a perfect pudding should be as spherical as possible, have an unblemished shiny coating and a dense, moist, flavoursome interior.

WARM BUTTER CAKE WITH PLUMS POACHED IN KIR

This butter cake is very rich and very moreish and can be made in advance. The plums also improve with keeping, making this an easy pudding for a dinner party (See Tip). Be warned, there will be requests for second helpings.

Serves 8

6 egg yolks

250g/9oz plain flour

190g/6½oz caster sugar

225g/8oz butter at room temperature and cut into small pieces, plus extra for greasing

FOR THE PLUMS

175g/6oz caster sugar

300ml/½ pint white wine

2 tbsp crème de cassis liqueur (kir)

900g/2lb (about 24) red-skinned or Victoria plums, halved and stoned

1 Preheat the oven to 190C/375F/Gas 5. Grease a 4cm/1½in deep, 25cm/10in flan tin with plenty of butter.

2 Lightly beat the egg yolks together in a small bowl. Sift the flour into a bowl and make a dip in the middle. Add almost all the egg yolks (reserving about one tablespoon for glazing the tart at the end), the sugar and the butter, and gradually mix the ingredients together until you have a smooth dough. Transfer to the tin and press out evenly using lightly floured hands, making sure that the top is smooth. Brush with the reserved egg yolk, then mark with a squiggly criss-cross pattern using the back of a fork. Bake for 15 minutes, then reduce the oven to 160C/325F/Gas 3 and bake for a further 15 minutes until the top is golden.

3 Meanwhile, for the plums, place the sugar and wine in a large pan and bring to the boil. Add the crème de cassis and the plums and simmer very gently for 1–2 minutes until just tender (this will depend on the ripeness of your plums). Lift the plums out of the syrup with a slotted spoon and transfer to a shallow dish. Boil the syrup for 5–6 minutes until it has reduced to a coating consistency. Cool a little, then pour back over the plums. This is quite important because if the syrup is too hot, it will continue to cook the plums even more, which you don't want. They must be served warm, not hot.

4 Leave the butter cake to cool in the tin for 15 minutes, then turn it out on to a wire rack. Serve warm, cut into wedges with the poached plums.

Nutrition notes per serving: *623 Calories, Protein 6g, Carbohydrate 83g, Fat 29g, Saturated fat 17g, Fibre 3g, Added sugar 48g, Salt 0.59g.*

TIP

Cook the butter cake a couple of days ahead and keep in an airtight tin. Cover the plums and keep in the fridge. Just before serving, simply warm the cake in an oven preheated to 160C/325F/Gas 3 for 10 minutes and heat the plums gently in a pan, but don't let them boil.

Chilled Puds

CHAMPAGNE JELLIES WITH A CITRUS FRUIT SALAD

These lovely translucent jellies look stunning with the multi-coloured citrus pieces floating in their passion fruit sea. I'm getting a bit carried away with the prose, but this is a refreshing and stylish way to end a meal.

Serves 4

250ml/9fl oz champagne or sparkling dry white wine

250g/9oz caster sugar

4 x 3g sheets leaf gelatine or 11g sachet powdered gelatine (See Tip)

FOR THE CITRUS FRUIT SALAD

12 passion fruit, halved

caster sugar, to taste

2 ruby grapefruit

2 oranges

1 lemon

1 lime

1   Make the jellies: place the champagne or sparkling wine and sugar in a pan and leave over a gentle heat until the sugar has dissolved. Meanwhile, if using leaf gelatine, soak in cold water for a few minutes until softened, then lift out and squeeze out excess water before stirring into the champagne mixture and leaving until dissolved. If using powdered gelatine, place three tablespoons of cold water in a pan, sprinkle over the powder and leave to sponge for 5 minutes. Heat very gently until clear, then stir into the champagne mixture. Pour into four wet dariole or mini-pudding moulds and leave to set in the fridge overnight.

2   The next day, make the citrus fruit salad. Scoop out the passion fruit pulp into a sieve, set over a small pan. Press out the juice with a wooden spoon and reserve a few of the seeds for decoration. Discard the remainder. Cook the juice over a gentle heat until it thickens, then stir in a little caster sugar to taste. Leave to go cold, cover and chill until needed.

3   Slice the top and bottom off each citrus fruit, then cut away all the skin and white pith with a small, sharp knife. Cut either side of each dividing membrane to remove the fruit in neat segments, then stir into the passion fruit juice.

4   Dip the jelly moulds very briefly in warm water, then turn the jellies out into the centres of four plates. Spoon round the citrus salad and sprinkle with the reserved passion fruit seeds.

Nutrition notes per serving: *411 Calories, Protein 6g, Carbohydrate 91g, Fat 1g, Saturated fat 0g, Fibre 4g, Added sugar 74g, Salt 0.05g.*

TIP

Gelatine leaves are a chef's dream and now that they are more readily available you should give them a try. There are no lumps to worry about, they are easy to use and they dissolve instantly.

MACERATED STRAWBERRIES

675–900g (1½–2lb) strawberries, hulled and halved if large

2 tbsp caster sugar

1 tbsp eau de fraise, eau de vie or Kirsch (See Tip)

12 fresh basil leaves, very finely shredded

1 Place the strawberries in a bowl with the sugar, eau de fraise, eau de vie or Kirsch and basil. Cover and chill in the fridge for 15–30 minutes.

Nutrition notes per serving for 6: *56 Calories, Protein 1g, Carbohydrate 12g, Fat trace, Saturated fat 0g, Fibre 1g, Added sugar 5g, Salt 0.02g.*

TIP

Eau de vie literally means 'water of life' and is the French name given to a number of fruit brandies. The best known include Kirsch (cherry) and fraise (strawberry). Kirsch is made in northeastern parts of France, such as Alsace and is often used as a flavouring in fruit compotes and other desserts.

CARAMELISED RICE PUDDING WITH A COMPOTE OF BLUEBERRIES

1 vanilla pod, split

600ml/1 pint milk

70g/2½oz caster sugar

55g/2oz pudding rice

125ml/4fl oz double cream

icing sugar, for dusting

FOR THE COMPOTE

250ml/9fl oz Stock syrup (page 62)

juice of ½ lemon

1 tbsp cassis (optional)

225g/8oz fresh blueberries

1 Place the vanilla pod, milk and sugar in a pan and bring slowly to the boil. Stir in the rice, bring back to the boil and simmer very gently for 1 hour or until thick and gooey. Remove the vanilla pod, leave the rice to cool, then chill.

2 Make the compote: bring the sugar syrup, lemon juice and cassis, if using, to the boil in a pan. Add the blueberries and simmer for 2 minutes, then pour into a bowl and leave to cool.

3 Preheat the grill to high. Whip the cream until it forms soft peaks and fold lightly into the cooled rice. Place a deep 6cm/2½in scone cutter on a baking sheet. Spoon in a quarter of the rice mixture, lightly level the top, then remove the cutter. Repeat to make three more. Dust heavily with icing sugar.

4 Caramelise the sugar under the grill or by very carefully using a blowtorch until it is bubbling and has turned a dark golden brown. Set aside to cool slightly, then slide a fish slice under each pudding and transfer to a serving plate. Spoon round the blueberry compote.

Nutrition notes per serving: *568 Calories, Protein 7g, Carbohydrate 94g, Fat 21g, Saturated fat 13g, Fibre 1g, Added sugar 72g, Salt 0.25g.*

CRÈME FRAÎCHE TERRINE WITH CALVADOS CREAM SAUCE AND CIDERED PEARS

A big slice of vanilla-flavoured mousse with caramelised pears and a Calvados and caramel cream sauce – need I say more? All right, don't eat too much in one sitting.

Serve 8–12

5 tsp powdered gelatine

450ml/16fl oz natural yogurt

200ml/7fl oz crème fraîche

85g/3oz caster sugar

150ml/¼ pint double cream

2 tsp vanilla extract

2 egg whites

FOR THE CALVADOS CREAM SAUCE

115g/4oz caster sugar

300ml/½ pint double cream

3 tbsp Calvados (See Tip, page 28), Pommeau or brandy

FOR THE CIDERED PEARS

4–6 dessert pears (See Tip)

40g/1½oz unsalted butter

3 tbsp caster sugar

3 tbsp dry cider

1 Place five tablespoons of cold water in a small pan. Sprinkle over the gelatine and leave to sponge for 5 minutes.

2 Mix together the yogurt, crème fraîche and sugar together in a large bowl until smooth. Lightly whip the cream until it begins to thicken and fold it into the yogurt mixture with the vanilla extract. Place the pan of gelatine over a low heat and leave until clear. Stir into the creamy mixture, making sure it is mixed well.

3 Whisk the egg whites until they form soft peaks – the tips of the peaks should flop over, not stand upright. Fold one large spoonful into the yogurt mixture to loosen it slightly, then gently fold in the remainder. Pour the mixture into a 7.5cm (3in) deep, 7.5 x 25cm (3 x 10in) terrine dish (or 900g/2lb loaf tin, lined with plastic wrap to avoid rusting), cover with plastic wrap and chill in the fridge for 6 hours or preferably overnight.

4 Make the Calvados cream: place the sugar and two tablespoons of water in a pan and stir over a high heat until the sugar has dissolved. Leave it to cook without stirring until it has turned a rich amber colour. Remove from the heat, pour in the cream and stir until all the caramel has dissolved into it – you might need to return it to a very low heat for 1–2 minutes. Remove from the heat, leave to cool, then stir in the Calvados.

5 Just before you are ready to serve, cook the pears. Cut the pears into quarters, remove the cores, then peel. Cut each piece in half once more. Melt the butter in a large, heavy-based frying pan and, as soon it starts to foam, add the pears and fry over a high heat for 1 minute on each side until golden brown. Sprinkle over the sugar and cider and cook for no more than 2 minutes until the cider has reduced and formed a sugary syrup with the butter and sugar.

6 Dip the terrine or loaf tin briefly into warm water. Invert on to a serving plate and cut into slices. Place a piece on each plate and arrange a few cidered pears alongside, then pour over the Calvados cream sauce and serve immediately.

Nutrition notes per serving for 8: *597 Calories, Protein 8g, Carbohydrate 47g, Fat 42g, Saturated fat 26g, Fibre 2g, Added sugar 33g, Salt 0.25g.*

TIP

Try to use ripe Comice pears for this dish. Comice are large and roundish pears with a yellow skin that has a greenish tinge, speckled and russetted, sometimes with a red blush. Their flesh is soft, creamy white, very juicy and full of flavour. Ripe pears 'give' a little at the stem end. Choose those with no oozing or softness.

SUMMER BERRY BRÛLÉE

The great thing about this is the lovely puddle of fruity caramel juices at the bottom of the pot, which soak into the custard.

Serves 6

85g/3oz granulated sugar, plus 6 heaped teaspoons

175g/6oz mixed prepared blueberries, blackcurrants and redcurrants

175g/6oz raspberries and halved small strawberries

1 vanilla pod, split

600ml/1 pint double cream

6 egg yolks

55g/2oz caster sugar

1 Place the granulated sugar in a heavy-based pan and cook over a medium heat until it dissolves and turns to a light brown caramel. Remove the pan from the heat, then stir in the blueberries, blackcurrants and redcurrants. The heat of the caramel will cook the fruit a little but the caramel will start to harden around them, so return to a low heat and warm gently until it has dissolved. Stir in the raspberries and strawberries and divide between six 7.5cm/3in ramekins.

2 Scrape the vanilla pod seeds into a pan. Add the cream and vanilla pod to the pan and slowly bring up to the boil. Place the egg yolks and caster sugar in a heatproof bowl, set over a pan of simmering water, then whisk until the mixture is very pale and thick.

3 Just before the cream boils over the sides of the pan, pour two-thirds on to the egg yolk mixture and whisk together. Pour the mixture back into the pan containing the remaining cream and stir over a low heat for 2–3 minutes until it is thick and coats the back of a spoon. Remove the pan from the heat and stir for 2 minutes. Remove the vanilla pod and pour the mixture into the ramekins, filling right to the top. Leave to set in the fridge for at least 6 hours and preferably overnight.

4 Preheat the grill to high. Sprinkle the top of the brûlées with the remaining 6 teaspoons of granulated sugar, making sure you take it right to the edges of the ramekins, and slide them under the grill for 2–3 minutes until the sugar has caramelised. Leave until the sugar topping has cooled and gone hard before serving.

Nutrition notes per serving: *640 Calories, Protein 5g, Carbohydrate 36g, Fat 54g, Saturated fat 32g, Fibre 2g, Added sugar 31g, Salt 0.12g.*

TIP

The secret of making brûlées that set in the fridge is to whisk the egg yolks over simmering water until a strand from the whisk will lie on the surface of the mixture. You also need to ensure that the cream is just about to boil over before pouring it on to the yolks. That way, the mix cooks out in seconds rather than the more usual 15 minutes of stirring. Always use a wooden spoon to stir the mix once it is back in the pan and use a side-to-side motion rather than a circular one. This moves the cream about more and prevents that scrambled egg thing happening in the bottom of the pan.

CAUTION! This recipe contains lightly cooked eggs.

LITTLE SCOTTISH BUTTERSCOTCH POTS WITH VIENNESE SHORTBREAD FINGERS

These little puds are like a cross between a crème brûlée (without the top) and a mousse. What makes them so special is the 'toffee', which you make by boiling a can of sweetened condensed milk until it caramelises inside the tin. All they then need is a thin layer of unwhipped cream flooded over the top. If you like, you can use the biscuits to scoop out the mixture. Yum!

Serves 6

200g can sweetened condensed milk (See Tip)

6 egg yolks

375ml/13fl oz double cream, plus extra to serve

FOR THE VIENNESE SHORTBREAD FINGERS

85g/3oz butter, slightly softened

25g/1oz icing sugar, plus extra for dusting

25g/1oz cornflour

55g/2oz plain flour

1 Place the unopened can of condensed milk in a pan and cover with cold water. Bring to the boil, then simmer for 3 hours, topping up the water every now and then so that it always covers the can. Leave to cool in the water.

2 Preheat the oven to 150C/300F/Gas 2. Open the can of 'toffee' and scrape it into a bowl. Stir in the egg yolks, then gradually stir in the cream until you have a smooth mixture. Strain into a jug, then pour it evenly into six 7.5cm/3in ramekins. Place in a roasting tin and pour in boiling water to come halfway up the sides of the ramekins. Cook for 20–25 minutes until just set but still a little wobbly. Remove from the tin, leave to cool, then cover and chill for at least 2 hours.

3 Meanwhile, make the biscuits: increase the oven to 180C/350F/Gas 4. Lightly grease and flour a baking sheet. Beat together the butter and sugar until pale and creamy. Sift the cornflour and flour together, then beat into the butter mixture until smooth. Spoon the mixture into a piping bag fitted with a large star nozzle and pipe twelve 7.5cm/3in fingers spaced well apart on to the baking sheet. Chill in the fridge for 30 minutes. Bake the biscuits for 10–12 minutes until golden. Leave to go cold, then carefully lift off the baking sheet.

4 Pour a thin layer of unwhipped cream on to the top of each butterscotch pot. Dust the shortbread fingers with a little icing sugar and serve beside the pots.

Nutrition notes per serving: *623 Calories, Protein 8g, Carbohydrate 36g, Fat 51g, Saturated fat 30g, Fibre trace, Added sugar 20g, Salt 0.48g.*

TIP

Condensed milk is pasteurised, homogenised milk that it boiled under special conditions until it is reduced to about a third of its original volume. Its texture is thick and viscous and its high sugar content acts as a preservative.

DRAMBUIE ORANGES

Serves 4

6–8 small juicy seedless
thin-skinned oranges

4 tbsp Drambuie

1   Slice the top and bottom off each orange and sit each one on a board. Cut away the outer skin so that there is no white pith left behind, then slice each orange across into thin slices. Arrange the slices overlapping on plates, drizzle over the Drambuie and serve.

2   Alternatively, place the orange slices in a shallow dish with the Drambuie, cover and leave to chill in the fridge for 3–4 hours, during which time the juice from the oranges will develop a wonderful tasting sauce. Arrange on serving plates and serve chilled.

Nutrition notes per serving: *89 Calories, Protein 2g, Carbohydrate 13g, Fat trace, Saturated fat 0g, Fibre 3g, Added sugar 0g, Salt 0.02g.*

CINNAMON CREAM WITH SPICED RHUBARB

Serves 8

700ml/1¼ pints double cream

1 cinnamon stick

½ tsp ground cinnamon

3 gelatine leaves

85g/3oz caster sugar

FOR THE SPICED RHUBARB

675g/1½ lb rhubarb (See Tip), cut
into 4cm/1½ in lengths

425g/15oz granulated sugar

1 cinnamon stick

3 star anise

6 cloves

1 vanilla pod

strip of pared lemon zest

1   Place the cream, cinnamon stick and ground cinnamon in a pan and bring to the boil. Remove from the heat and stand for 20 minutes to infuse the flavour.

2   Meanwhile, soak the gelatine leaves in cold water for 10 minutes until softened and squeeze to remove excess water. Bring the cream to just below boiling point once more. Add the caster sugar and the gelatine and stir until they have both dissolved. Strain the mixture into a jug to remove the cinnamon stick, then pour into eight 90ml/3fl oz dariole moulds or individual yogurt cartons. Leave overnight in the fridge to set.

3   For the rhubarb: place 450ml/16fl oz water and the sugar in a large pan and bring slowly to the boil, stirring now and then until the sugar has dissolved. Add the spices, vanilla pod and lemon zest and simmer for 5 minutes. Add the rhubarb, bring back to the boil and simmer gently for 2 minutes. Remove the pan from the heat and leave to cool.

4   Run a sharp knife round the top of the mould, dip the bottom very briefly into warm water, turn upside down into the palm of your hand and shake to loosen. Unmould on to plates and spoon round the rhubarb.

Nutrition notes per serving: *683 Calories, Protein 3g, Carbohydrate 70g, Fat 45g, Saturated fat 28g, Fibre 1g, Added sugar 67g, Salt 0.09g.*

TIP

This cinnamon cream is really just panna cotta (an Italian set cream), flavoured with cinnamon instead of vanilla. We serve this pudding in early summer when the first pale-pink forced rhubarb arrives. If you're using the later, main-crop rhubarb, you may need to peel it before slicing and cook for a little longer. Both the cream and rhubarb can be made up to 2 days in advance.

Chocolate Delights

FROZEN CHOCOLATE CAKE ❄

One from my pal Jim Kerr (chef, not singer), who is now the general manager of my new Glasgow restaurant, Nairns. The chocolate cake is very tasty and a little goes a long way. The mascarpone helps it slip down a treat.

Serves 8

200g/7oz bitter plain chocolate, broken into pieces (See Tip)

200g/7oz caster sugar

200g/7oz unsalted butter

150ml/¼ pint espresso coffee or 2 tsp instant coffee dissolved in 150ml/¼ pint water

3 eggs

FOR THE MASCARPONE

250g/9oz mascarpone

1 tbsp caster sugar

1 egg yolk

1 Preheat the oven to 180C/350F/Gas 4. Line a 20 x 30cm (8 x 12in) shallow rectangular baking tin with non-stick baking paper.

2 Make the cake: place the chocolate, sugar, butter and espresso in a pan and leave over a low heat for 5 minutes or until everything has melted, then increase the heat a little and allow the mixture to come up to a gentle simmer. Simmer for 10 minutes, stirring frequently, until the mixture has slightly caramelised, then leave to cool slightly.

3 Break the eggs into a bowl and whisk together lightly. Slowly pour in the caramelised chocolate mixture and keep whisking for 2 minutes until the mixture turns very glossy. Strain through a sieve into the tin and bake for 30 minutes until firm to the touch. Cool, remove from the tin, then transfer to the freezer and leave for 6 hours until it has just frozen, but not so that it is rock hard.

4 Meanwhile, beat the mascarpone with the caster sugar and egg yolk until thick. Cover and chill in the fridge. Remove the cake from the freezer and lift it out of the tin. Peel back the baking paper and cut the cake in half lengthways, then across into four so that you end up with eight rectangular pieces. Serve with the mascarpone.

Nutrition notes per serving: *598 Calories, Protein 5g, Carbohydrate 46g, Fat 45g, Saturated fat 27g, Fibre 0g, Added sugar 43g, Salt 0.16g.*

TIP

Use plain chocolate that contains more than 65 per cent cocoa solids for this and other dark chocolate puddings in this book. You'll find the percentage stated on the packaging.

LAYERED WHITE AND DARK CHOCOLATE MOUSSE

You can either serve these mousses layered up in tall glasses or sandwich them together between discs of plain chocolate.

FOR THE DARK CHOCOLATE MOUSSE

165g/5½ oz good-quality plain chocolate, broken into pieces (See Tip, page 51)

3 egg yolks

5 egg whites

55g/2oz caster sugar

FOR THE WHITE CHOCOLATE MOUSSE

1 gelatine leaf

175g/6oz white chocolate, broken into pieces (See Tip)

2 egg yolks

250ml/9fl oz double cream

2 egg whites

FOR THE CHOCOLATE DISCS (OPTIONAL)

300g/10½ oz good-quality plain chocolate

icing sugar, for dusting

1   If making the discs, break 200g/7oz of the plain chocolate into a heatproof bowl, set over a pan of barely simmering water, making sure the bowl is not touching the water. Leave until melted, then remove the bowl from the pan and break in the remaining chocolate and stir until it melts. Depending on your kitchen (it has to be cool), lightly oil a smooth work surface or a large, chilled baking sheet. Cover with plastic wrap, pour on the chocolate and spread it out in a thin layer with a palette knife. Cool or put in the fridge to set. Cut the chocolate into 7.5cm/3in discs using a plain pastry cutter or cut into squares with a knife. Lift off the plastic wrap and set aside in a single layer, to cool.

2   For the dark chocolate mousse: melt the chocolate in a heatproof bowl set over a pan of barely simmering water. Cool slightly, then beat in the egg yolks until the mixture is smooth and coming away from the sides of the bowl. In a large bowl, whisk the egg whites until soft peaks form, then gradually whisk in the sugar, making sure the mixture doesn't get too stiff. Stir a quarter of the egg whites into the chocolate to loosen the mixture slightly, then gently fold in the remainder. Cover and chill in the fridge.

3   For the white chocolate mousse: soak the gelatine in water for 10 minutes. Set a bowl over a pan of barely simmering water until it is warm, add the chocolate, take the pan off the heat and set aside until the chocolate has melted. Squeeze out excess water from the gelatine, then beat it into the chocolate with the egg yolks. The mixture will look as if it has split at first but just keep beating and it will come back together and go smooth. In two bowls, whisk the cream and egg whites into soft peaks. Fold the cream into the chocolate mixture, followed by the egg whites.

4   Now either alternate layers of dark and white mousse in eight tall glasses and chill overnight or, if layering the discs, cover the mousses and chill overnight. Just before serving, place a chocolate disc/square on each plate and top with a spoonful of the dark mousse. Cover with another disc, then add some white mousse. Top with a final layer of chocolate and dust with icing sugar.

Nutrition notes per serving: *638 Calories, Protein 10g, Carbohydrate 59g, Fat 42g, Saturated fat 21g, Fibre 0g, Added sugar 41g, Salt 0.26g.*

TIP

Don't let white chocolate get too hot or it will go grainy and is then difficult to work with. White chocolate is made from cocoa butter and milk products. With a high cocoa butter content it is expensive and has a fine flavour. Cheaper types have a different, sweet flavour. High quality white chocolate does not store well and should be used within about 3 months, otherwise it can taste rancid.

CAUTION! This recipe contains raw eggs.

CHOCOLATE ORANGE CHEESECAKE

Not surprisingly, the inspiration for this came from eating a Terry's Chocolate orange. It's made with easily accessible ingredients. To save time, you could omit one of the sauces.

Serves 4

3 oranges

55g/2oz butter, melted

½ tsp ground mixed spice

½ tsp ground cinnamon (See Tip)

115g/4oz digestive biscuits, crushed

225g/8oz good-quality plain chocolate, broken into pieces (See Tip, page 51)

115g/4oz caster sugar, plus 2 tsp

225g/8oz full fat cream cheese

150ml/¼ pint double cream

3 tbsp brandy

1 tsp cornflour

3 tbsp milk

1 tbsp cocoa powder, for dusting

1 Finely grate the zest from half of one of the oranges. Place all but one tablespoon of the melted butter in a bowl with the mixed spice, cinnamon, crushed biscuits and orange zest and mix together well. Place four 10cm/4in scone cutters on a baking sheet. Divide the crumbs between the rings and press down lightly. Brush the sides of the rings with the remaining melted butter.

2 Melt the chocolate in a bowl set over a pan of barely simmering water. Pare the zest from the remaining two oranges with a potato peeler. Cut the strips into fine matchsticks. Place the 115g/4oz of sugar in a pan with 125ml/4fl oz of water and leave over a low heat until the sugar has completely dissolved. Bring to the boil, add the fine matchsticks and simmer for 10 minutes.

3 Meanwhile, place the cream cheese in a bowl and whisk until smooth, Beat in half the melted chocolate. Pour the cream into a bowl and whip until it forms soft peaks. Whisk in two tablespoons of the brandy and one teaspoon of the remaining sugar. Gently fold into the cream cheese mixture, then spoon into the metal rings. Place in the freezer for 15 minutes or in the fridge until firm.

4 Strain the orange syrup through a sieve into a bowl, reserving the zest matchsticks. Squeeze the juice from two of the oranges and place in a small pan with the cornflour. Bring to the boil, whisking all the time and simmer for 1 minute until thickened. Stir in two tablespoons of the orange syrup (either discard the remainder or store in a jar in the fridge for another occasion). Spread the orange matchsticks over a plate and sprinkle with the remaining sugar and toss lightly until well coated.

5 Stir the milk and remaining brandy into the remaining melted chocolate. If you like, cut the peel and pith off the last orange and remove the flesh in segments.

6 Remove the cheesecakes from the fridge and transfer to a plate using a palette knife. Briefly warm the outside of each ring with a warm, wet cloth and remove. Dust the top of each one with sifted cocoa powder, then pile the orange matchsticks on top. Drizzle the orange and chocolate sauces around each cheesecake and decorate the plates with orange segments if you like.

Nutrition notes per serving: *1154 Calories, Protein 9g, Carbohydrate 102g, Fat 79g, Saturated fat 48g, Fibre 3g, Added sugar 70g, Salt 1.28g.*

TIP

Cinnamon, a popular spice with a sweet, pungent flavour, goes particularly well with chocolate dishes. It is the inner bark of a small evergreen tree grown mostly in Sri Lanka. As well as being available ground, it can be bought as sticks or quills and, in its more natural state, as rough pieces of bark.

SOFT CHOCOLATE CAKE WITH MASCARPONE CREAM AND ESPRESSO COFFEE SAUCE

You might as well ask me to list the moons of Jupiter as name my favourite pudding. This one comes close, though. It's as rich and moist as any chocolate cake I've ever tasted. Coffee and cream have a special affinity, and all these ingredients sit well together. I use espresso coffee as much for its aroma as its flavour. The mascarpone cream could be replaced with ordinary whipped cream or chocolate sauce.

Serves 8

225g/8oz unsalted butter

225g/8oz good-quality plain chocolate, broken into pieces (See Tip, page 51)

140g/5oz caster sugar

6 egg yolks

8 egg whites

Caramel twists (See Tip), to decorate (optional)

sifted icing sugar, to decorate

FOR THE MASCARPONE CREAM

175g/6oz mascarpone

25g/1oz caster sugar

50ml/2fl oz double cream

FOR THE ESPRESSO COFFEE SAUCE

6 egg yolks

85g/3oz caster sugar

600ml/1 pint milk

50ml/2fl oz extra strong espresso coffee or 1 tsp espresso granules dissolved in 50ml/2fl oz hot water

2 tbsp Kahlua liqueur

icing sugar, for dusting

1 Preheat the oven to 160C/325F/Gas 3. Lightly butter a 25cm/10in springform cake tin, then line the base with non-stick baking paper.

2 Set a heatproof bowl over a pan of simmering water and melt the butter and chocolate together until smooth. Remove and set aside. Whisk together the sugar and egg yolks until pale and thick and the whisk leaves a trail on the surface for a few seconds. Gently fold into the melted chocolate.

3 Whisk the egg whites into soft peaks – the tips of the peaks should just fold over, not stand upright. Very gently fold the whites into the chocolate mixture. Pour into the tin and bake for 45 minutes. It will soufflé up during cooking and just crack when it's ready but then collapse once you bring it out of the oven. Don't worry, this is just the way it should be. Cool in the tin.

4 Make the mascarpone cream: beat the mascarpone and caster sugar together until smooth, then gradually whisk in the double cream. Cover and chill.

5 Make the espresso sauce: whisk together the egg yolks and sugar until thick and creamy. Bring the milk to the boil in a small pan, then whisk into the egg yolks. Pour the mixture back into the pan and cook over a gentle heat, stirring constantly, until thick enough to coat the back of a wooden spoon lightly. Stir in the coffee and liqueur and cool. Cover and chill until needed.

6 Remove the cake from the tin and peel off the paper. Cut into wedges and place on serving plates. Dredge with icing sugar and push in a caramel twist. Serve with the mascarpone cream and pour the espresso sauce around.

Nutrition notes per serving: *774 Calories, Protein 12g, Carbohydrate 58g, Fat 56g, Saturated fat 32g, Fibre 0g, Added sugar 51g, Salt 0.37g.*

TIP

To make Caramel twists: line a baking sheet with foil. Heat 115g/4oz granulated sugar and 30ml/1fl oz water in a pan over a low heat until clear. Boil rapidly until it turns dark. Plunge the base of the pan into cold water to arrest cooking and quickly drizzle tight swirls of caramel from a spoon on to the baking sheet. Leave to set, then peel off and use for decoration.

CAUTION! This recipe contains lightly cooked eggs.

Ice Cream

CINNAMON ICE CREAM ✳

Serves 6

600ml/1 pint milk
1½ lightly crushed cinnamon sticks
6 egg yolks
70g/2½oz caster sugar
125ml/4fl oz double cream

1 Place the milk and cinnamon sticks in a pan and bring slowly to the boil. Remove from the heat and leave for 20 minutes for the flavours to infuse.

2 Whisk the egg yolks and sugar together in a bowl until pale and creamy. Bring the milk back to the boil, lift out the cinnamon sticks and whisk the milk into the egg yolks mixture. Return the mixture to the pan and cook over a gentle heat, stirring constantly, until it thickens enough to coat the back of a wooden spoon. (This shouldn't take more than 3 minutes.) Stir in the double cream and leave to cool. Cover and place in the fridge until well chilled.

3 Churn the mixture in an ice cream maker or pour into a shallow plastic box and freeze until almost firm. Scrape into a food processor and whizz until smooth. Pour it back into the box, return to the freezer and freeze until firm. Repeat.

Nutrition notes per serving: *263 Calories, Protein 7g, Carbohydrate 17g, Fat 19g, Saturated fat 10g, Fibre 0g, Added sugar 11g, Salt 0.18g.*

TIP

Ice cream should really be churned and eaten on the same day. If it has been made in advance, soften in the fridge for 30 minutes before serving.

CAUTION! This recipe contains lightly cooked eggs.

TUILE CONES ✳

Makes 8–10

25g/1oz caster sugar
25g/1oz plain flour
1 egg white
25g/1oz unsalted butter, melted

1 Preheat the oven to 180C/350F/Gas 4. Lightly grease a baking sheet. Place the sugar, flour and egg white in a bowl and beat together to a smooth paste. Beat in the melted butter, then cover and chill in the fridge for 20 minutes.

2 Drop about three teaspoons of the mixture well apart on to the baking sheet and spread out thinly into 13cm/5in circles. Bake for 6–8 minutes until golden around the edges. Remove from the oven, cool for a few seconds, then, working quickly, lift each one off the baking sheet with a palette knife and roll into a cone shape. Leave to cool and harden. Repeat to make remaining cones.

Nutrition notes per serving for 8: *38 Calories, Protein 1g, Carbohydrate 3g, Fat 3g, Saturated fat 2g, Fibre trace, Added sugar 1g, Salt 0.08g.*

✳ *Keep cones in the fridge for up to 1 week or freezer for up to 2 months.*

STRAWBERRY ICE CREAM IN BRANDY SNAP BASKETS ✹

Home-made ice cream is always a big hit and if you have an ice-cream maker all you have to do is bung in the correct ingredients at the correct time. This is a coarse ice cream, with plenty of strawberry pieces running through it.

Serves 4

FOR THE ICE CREAM

600ml/1 pint milk

6 egg yolks

85g/3oz caster sugar

115g/4oz strawberries, hulled and halved, if large

FOR THE BRANDY SNAPS

25g/1oz butter

25g/1oz caster sugar

25g/1oz golden syrup

25g/1oz plain flour

FOR THE STRAWBERRY SAUCE

115g/4oz fresh strawberries

50ml/2fl oz Stock syrup (page 62)

1 Make the ice cream: bring the milk to the boil. Meanwhile, whisk the egg yolks and sugar together in a bowl until pale and creamy. Pour the boiling milk into the egg yolks mixture and whisk. Return the mixture to the pan and cook over a gentle heat, stirring constantly, until it thickens enough to coat the back of a wooden spoon. (This shouldn't take more than 3 minutes.) Leave to cool. Cover and place in the fridge until well chilled.

2 You can either churn the mixture in an ice cream maker, adding the strawberries halfway through churning, or pour it into a shallow plastic box and freeze until almost firm. Scrape the mixture into a food processor and whizz until smooth. Pour it back into the box, then return to the freezer and freeze until firm. Repeat once more. Add the strawberries after its last whizz in the food processor. Transfer to the fridge 30 minutes before serving to soften slightly.

3 Make the brandy snaps: melt the butter, sugar, and golden syrup together, then beat in the flour. Leave to cool, then chill in the fridge until firm. Scoop it on to a large sheet of plastic wrap and shape into a 2.5cm/1in thick roll. Wrap firmly in the plastic wrap and chill until really hard.

4 Preheat the oven to 200C/400F/Gas 6. Lightly oil a baking sheet. Cut four 5mm/¼in slices off the roll and place well spaced apart on the baking sheet. Return any that is not being used to the fridge or it will go soft. Bake for 5 minutes or until richly golden. Remove from the oven and leave on the baking sheet for 1 minute. Lift off with a palette knife and drape each one over an upturned egg cup to form a little basket. Remove when set.

5 Make the sauce: push the strawberries through a sieve with the back of a spoon and add the Stock syrup. Place a scoop of ice cream in each brandy snap basket and drizzle round the sauce.

Nutrition notes per serving: *440 Calories, Protein 10g, Carbohydrate 60g, Fat 19g, Saturated fat 9g, Fibre 1g, Added sugar 44g, Salt 0.42g.*

TIP

The brandy snap mixture keeps well, refrigerated, for a week or freezes well for up to 2 months. Any leftover cooked brandy snaps keep well in an airtight tin.

CAUTION! This recipe contains lightly cooked eggs.

Basics

SWEET PASTRY

Makes enough to line one
25cm/10in tart tin or six
10cm/4in tartlet tins

**175g/6oz unsalted butter, diced
and chilled**

55g/2oz caster sugar

pinch of salt

250g/9oz plain flour

1 egg yolk

1 Place the butter, sugar and salt together in a food processor and whizz for 20 seconds until light and slightly broken up. Add one tablespoon of the flour and give a quick pulse. Add the egg yolk and briefly pulse, then add all the remaining flour and whizz until the mixture resembles big breadcrumbs. Add one tablespoon of cold water and whizz for 15 seconds until it forms a soft dough.

2 Turn the dough out on to a lightly floured surface and knead briefly until smooth. Wrap in plastic wrap and chill in the fridge for at least 2–3 hours before using.

CRÈME ANGLAISE

Makes 600ml/1 pint

600ml/1 pint milk

1 split vanilla pod

6 egg yolks

70g/2½oz caster sugar

1 Place the milk and vanilla pod in a pan and bring to the boil. Remove from the heat and leave to infuse for 20 minutes.

2 Whisk the egg yolks and sugar together until pale and creamy. Remove the vanilla pod and whisk the hot milk into the yolks. Return to the pan and cook over a gentle heat, stirring constantly, until it thickens enough to coat the back of a wooden spoon lightly. It is now ready to eat.

CAUTION! This recipe contains lightly cooked eggs.

STOCK SYRUP

Makes 1.3 litres/2¼ pints

1 kg/2¼ lb granulated sugar

1 Place the sugar and 1 litre/1¾ pints water in a medium-sized pan over a high heat. Bring to the boil, stirring from time to time. Simmer for about 5 minutes before skimming off any impurities that may have risen to the surface. Cool and use as required. It keeps for 8 weeks in the fridge.

INDEX

INDEX

Many of your favourite TV Cooks are also featured in a range of specially filmed half-hour BBC videos. They share the secrets of their key techniques and demonstrate some of their favourite recipes. Each video contains detailed step-by-step instructions on how to prepare and present creative dishes, acting as a companion to the book series.

The following are available as books and videos or as combined packs:

Ken Hom Cooks Chinese	BBCV5994
Mary Berry Cooks Cakes	BBCV6381
Mary Berry Cooks Puddings & Desserts	BBCV6193
Michael Barry Cooks Crafty Classics	BBCV6115
Nick Nairn Cooks The Main Course	BBCV6380
Rick Stein Cooks Fish	BBCV6111
Sophie Grigson Cooks Vegetables	BBCV6112
Valentina Harris Cooks Italian	BBCV6117

The following are only available as books:

Antonio Carluccio Cooks Pasta	0 563 38455 7
Keith Floyd Cooks Barbies	0 563 38346 1
Ken Hom Cooks Noodles and Rice	0 563 38454 9
Madhur Jaffrey Cooks Curries	0 563 38794 7
Rick Stein Cooks Seafood	0 563 38453 0